Guess What

Published in the United States of America by
Cherry Lake Publishing
Ann Arbor, Michigan
www.cherrylakepublishing.com

Reading Adviser: Marla Conn MS, Ed., Literacy specialist, Read-Ability, Inc.
Book Designer: Felicia Macheske

Photo Credits: © © Lepas/Shutterstock.com, cover; © Eric Isselee/Shutterstock.com, 1, 4, 11, back cover; © Igor Kovalchuk/
Shutterstock.com, 3; Natalia7/Shutterstock.com, 7; © hasan eroglu/Shutterstock.com, 8; © Meisterdragon/Shutterstock.com, 12;
© PrakapenkaAlena/Shutterstock.com, 15; © Roman Sigaev/Shutterstock.com, 17; © Nadiia Diachenko/Shutterstock.com, 18;
© Andrey_Kuzmin/Shutterstock.com, back cover

Library of Congress Cataloging-in-Publication Data has been filed and is available at catalog.loc.gov

Cherry Lake Publishing would like to acknowledge the work of The Partnership for 21st Century Skills.
Please visit *www.p21.org* for more information.

Printed in the United States of America
Corporate Graphics

Table of Contents

Hints **4-2I**

About **22**

**Things to
Think About** **23**

Glossary **24**

Index **24**

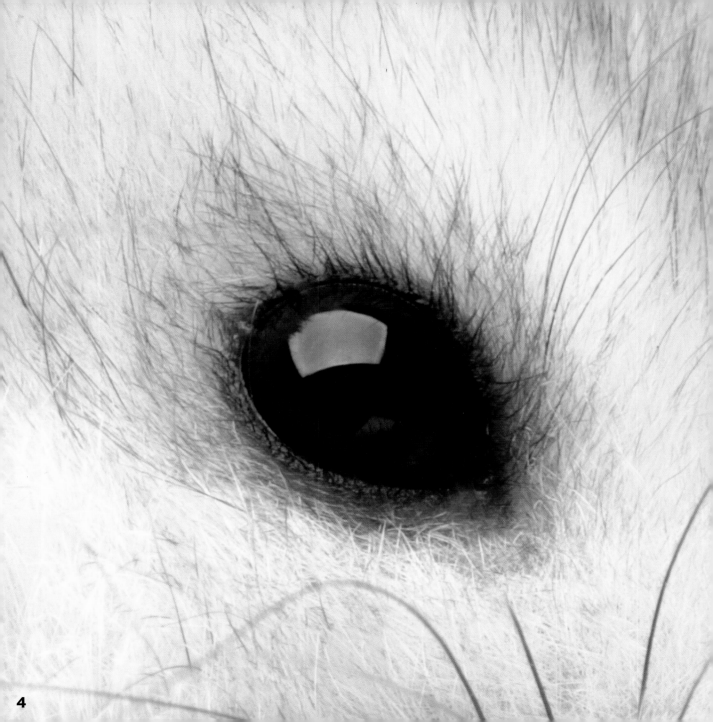

I can't see very well.

I can carry food in my cheeks.

I like to chew on things.

My body is covered with fur.

I come from a big family.

I like to exercise.

I use my **whiskers** to **feel** things.

I'm afraid of cats. Yikes!

Do you know what I am?

I'm a Hamster!

About Hamsters

1. Hamsters live about **4** years.

2. Hamsters can give birth to more than **20** babies at once.

3. Hamsters can learn to know you by your **smell**.

4. Hamsters use the pouches in their cheeks to carry food.

5. Hamster's front teeth grow all the time. They chew to **grind** them down.

Things to Think About
Before You Get a Pet

1. Can you take care of a pet for its whole life?

2. Do you have the money and the time to care for a pet?

3. Could you **adopt** a pet from a **rescue shelter**?

4. Do you have space in your home for a pet?

5. Can you keep a pet safe?

6. Can you keep other animals and people safe from a pet?

Glossary

adopt (uh-DOHPT) to bring an animal into your family

grind (GRINDE) to wear down or shorten by rubbing together

rescue shelter (RES-kyoo SHEL-tur) a place where an animal that was in danger or was not wanted can stay

smell (SMEL) to sense an odor with your nose

whiskers (WIS-kurz) long, stiff hairs near the mouth of some animals

Index

afraid, 19

cheeks, 6, 22
chew, 9, 22

exercise, 14

family, 13
feel, 16
food, 6, 22
fur, 10

live, 22

see, 5
smell, 22

teeth, 22

whiskers, 16